The poet is an introvert, but not really.
He reaches out to every parcel of the planet,
because everything is subject to him
(he delights in this double meaning).

— *Jon Obermeyer*

But This Comes Instead

**Poems
By**

S. R. Duncan

Box 5 – 720 – 6th St.,
New Westminster, BC
V3C 3C5   CANADA

TITLE: But This Comes Instead
AUTHOR: S. R. Duncan
Cover Photo: "Paris Catacombs" courtesy of S. R. Duncan
© 2018 Silver Bow Publishing

Library and Archives Canada Cataloguing in Publication

Duncan, S. R., 1965-, author
     But this comes instead : poems / by S. R. Duncan.

Issued in print and electronic formats.
ISBN 978-1-77403-008-0 (softcover).--ISBN 978-1-77403-009-7 (PDF)

     I. Title.

PS8557.U53745B88 2018   C811'.54   C2018-906542-7

                                                    C2018-906543-5

Silver Bow Publishing
Box 5 - 720 Sixth St.,
New Westminster, BC
CANADA V3L 3C5

Email: info@silverbowpublishing.com
Website: www.silverbowpublishing.com

**To the love of my life,
Catherine McCambridge.**

You are my poetry.

Acknowledgements

Thank you to Candice James and Ken Ader at Silver Bow Publishing for believing in my work enough to produce this book. Thank you, as well, to Bonnie Nish for supporting me in so many ways over the years. Thank you also to my friends Carol Anne McMillan and Peter Valentine for being my long-time comrades in arms.

Table of Contents

But This Comes Instead ... 11
They Burn Music Halls, Don't They? ... 14
"The Future Is Wide Open" - *for Tom* ... *20*
Breath ... 22
A Moment for Jake ... 26
Everyone Has a Poem About Cancer ... 29
The Dead of Winter ... 33
Bundled Ugliness ... 36
The Garbage Fairy ... 40
Likely It'll Happen ... 46
When Something Happened ... 50
Mill Town Gunslinger ... 56
The Dishwasher's Hour ... 61
Lady Hare Holding Greyhound ... 65
That First Quiet Year ... 67
A Day Counted in Crows ... 71
A Sparrow Death ... 72
This Brilliant Day ... 80
Party Like It's the End of the World ... 82

*"I see the beauty in you, and the darkness.
Both are brilliant."*

— Christina Strigas

But This Comes Instead

There are too many
tepid moments
like this one:
my heart
beating
unnoticed in its cage,
my neck sore
from holding my fat head up,
my mind out the window
with the shoplifter caught
on Main street,
feeling trapped,
traffic pretending
to go somewhere,
me believing it.

I sit down
to poke my fingers
into the un-giving night,
to pull out plums
to sweeten the taste
of warm blood;
to perfume the stale breath
of indifference
that lingers in my room
when the door remains closed;
to give
the silence
a voice.

But this old tenement
is far from paradise
and the cherry blossom confetti
has turned brown
under foot;
and the hookers curse
the rip-off station wagon
driving away.

And the old inspirations
are lost on me tonight:
the moon is dead.
So are the stars.
The mountains are out of reach
and the seasons are all the same mud.
My muse comes
empty-handed,
full of excuses,
angry,
telling me to fuck off
and stop calling.

There are times
when that rage
suits me well:
when I bang away
ham-fisted;
when the words
are black bruises
on the white of page.

But tonight,
I just wanted
to write a love poem,
the kind
you can't help but
smile at.
Simple;
heady with flowers;
warm with sunsets;
something safe
to send home to mother;
no skeletons
dragged out and dangled
in front of the neighbors;
something
to take me out of my dirty underwear,
my roach-infested nightmares,
all the awkward situations

I can't bring myself to leave;
out of my loveless, needy life.

I wanted to romance myself,
to pull the wool over my own eyes
and bask
in the gentle deception
of a pretty flood of words;
my day at the beach;
my time in the sun.

But this comes instead:
a slow,
dull
trickle
of blood;
pennies in the pockets
of my cheeks,
the mumbled discontent
of someone
who has bitten his tongue
before saying
what he
really wanted to say.

They Burn Music Halls, Don't They?

There is a smell particular
to a building gutted by fire.
It isn't what you might expect,
not rich and a little sad
like firewood burning,
but rancid,
as if memories
had a skin to them
that wasn't meant to burn.

From a block away
the stink of this death is on me,
up my nose and in my throat,
the feel of a dry heave
on a hungover morning,
already stale
in the late afternoon rain
only a day after
its blazing demise.
And it's hard to figure
how anything can burn
in this sloppy weather,
but the impossible proof
is right in front of me
like Noah's ark
on the side of Mt. Pleasant.

The Glass Slipper -
home to all that crazy jazz
and manic poetry,
and before that,
decades of jubilant gospel
and all the clamor of
people
full of food and prayer
and religious fervor -
is nothing
but a purple, clapboard shell,

its church-door mouth
already silenced
by a plywood gag.

The roof is gone.
It must have fallen in
on itself,
like a ribcage
unable to bear
the weight of the world
anymore.
Some nights you could sit upstairs -
close to the peak -
and imagine
the words and notes
perched in the rafters,
a million chattering birds
still finding sanctuary
though religion
had long left the building.
I want to be romantic and say
that now there's nothing between
those sounds
and heaven.
But with this endless suffering
of rain
threatening not to stop anytime soon,
I just can't get behind
that kind of lofty imagery.

And reality comes on slow
as does shock to the body,
There will be no more music.
The horns and harps and drums
will not sound.
The poets will talk,
will mourn,
but will ultimately go quiet;
all of us, musicians and poets alike,
shrugging our shoulders

in defeat
like everyone does
when something
we thought permanent
is taken from us,
us seeing no recourse,
standing small,
and naked
and alone.

And it's only because
I've been inside,
been a part of its history,
was just there earlier in the week,
that I take this tragedy personally.
But to look around
is to see hell cooled down:
the house at Fraser and 10th;
the apartment at 10th and Guelph;
the Main Street Dance Space;
the house on 10th and St. George;
half of Hastings Street
for Christ's sake;
some faring better than others,
the heart still in the ashes,
rising up again
like a resilient phoenix;
most bulldozed over
or left like rotting teeth
in a ragged smile;
every place
meaning something to somebody.

Is East Vancouver
burning down around us?
One spot fire at a time,
scattered over long stretches
of disassociation
so eyebrows
won't be raised,

so outcries
don't go up,
so we don't put
our solitary heads together
and for once
act like a community
and not just a polling district.

I ain't one for conspiracies.
Unless you call apathy one,
in which case we're all in on the plot!
No,
the perpetrators
might be
shadowy figures
with dubious intent,
or above them
prominent figures
with shadowy intent.
but the real villains
aren't doing anything.
Their doors are shut.
Their TVs are on too loud.
They are ignoring the alarms.
When the call goes out
to make changes,
they make excuses instead.

And even if it were a cigarette,
like the papers suggested,
the fact
that we let something
as serious as fire
slip through our fingers
and down
into the seat cushions
only goes
to prove my point:
We don't care enough.

This isn't a poem
that offers up
easy resolution -
rely on newscasters
and politicians
if you want
pat answers.
I'm as dumbstruck as anyone else -
another helpless,
stammering poet
who can't help thinking
he has one less stage
to strut across.

No,
this poem
is an invitation
to take the rage
which is
the next
certain step of grief
and use it
like a kick
in our own pants,
to maybe
go out and ask
a few pointed questions
of those who may know something
or who simply
hadn't thought much about it
before now;
to stand when called,
to do anything
but sit still
and gossip
like old men
fearing the snap
of their delicate bones
under the strain
of daunting challenge;

to learn enough
about the places
where we
sleep
and eat
and laugh
and work
and walk past
and look in
and mill about
and stand in line
that they become
more than strangers;
that our streets become
more than cold pavement
and the shortest distance
between here and there;
that, even if our neighborhood
is burning down
around our ears,
it won't go out forgotten;
that we will dance bravely
at its wake,
putting it down gentle,
gathering courage and resolve
to go on
despite its discouraging ashes.

*The Glass Slipper was an early 1990s Vancouver jazz club and one
of the key venues for improvisational and jazz music in the city.
Created as a practice venue with occasional concerts, The Glass
Slipper quickly became a venue for concerts seven nights a week,
featuring performances by local stars such as Claude Ranger,
Christopher Sigerson, Renee Doruyter and Peggy Lee. After an
arson in 1997, the venue operated by Ron Samworth and other
musicians did not reopen.*

"The Future is Wide Open"
- for Tom

What profound and awesome
optimism and fatalism
are forged into this double-edged sword of a lyric.
And whether we are seventeen years old
and staring down the business end of the Ventura Highway;
or eighty and standing in front of a pile of shattered bricks -
our past unceremoniously interred beneath;
or fifty-two and sitting comfortably numb in an armchair -
the luxury of time
and peace
is a banquet
stretched out
before us,
the irony of the ambiguity
is not lost on us.

I am caught up
in the sweet sad recollection
of whatever I imagine
my safe space used to be.
Each and every day we wake up
only half sure what will come of it,
despite our best efforts to attempt to control it.

The future is an unrehearsed moment,
an iceberg glance,
an awkward encounter,
a small bird
with young wings wide open
flying
(or falling)
for the first time.

It is standing on a beach,
our first time in open water.

And moments are spent
waiting for moments to happen
and regretting when they do
and regretting when they don't
and pining for the people who never call
and suffering those who do.

The future is as full of potential
as it is of inevitability.

We are all agoraphobic,
afraid of open spaces -
and the future is the widest
open
of them all.

Breath

In the beginning,
the lesson of respiration
is beaten into us
as we dangle
like the fish out of water
we are.
We cry with our very first breath.

In the beginning of the end
my mother's feet
wept
as if possessed of
some twisted sort of stigmata -
her body breaking down,
shedding
inconsolable, incurable
tears,
unable to contain
its suffering anymore.

When I took her arm
my hand went right down to bone -
bone ready
for the devil's pan pipe,
bone as brittle
as a winter's day.

I took her arm
and the truth of this sickness
sank into me,
real for the first time,
my hands wrapping too firmly around it,
her wincing because of me,
because I'd expected more to be there,
more to hold on to,
maybe believing
my bully weight

could finally do some good -
could pull her back up safe, alive.

And her life
in the end
was the story
of a mind unwilling
to give in to a body decaying.
That's how she was,
her strength
not in her muscle
(her muscle now clearly gone),
but from some place deeper,
a place ready to accept
whatever life threw at it,
and by accepting it,
somehow laughing it down,
triumphant in the face of it;
brave through years of prairie hardship
through the loss of son and spouse
brave when this disease came,
when none of her children could admit,
could scarce comprehend,
the hold it had on her,
brave,
even in sleep,
sleep a moment by moment
struggle
for a shallow, burning taste of air,
all those years
breath
simply given away
on the backs of words,
on the notes of songs,
on the snuffing of another year's candle,
breath
now something
we her children had to manage
on her behalf
like all her other affairs.

And so,
the oxygen man cometh,
blood pressure cuff in hand,
dressed like he delivered
bottled water instead,
monitoring condition
and updating her account
with his company
in the same
casual,
cold transaction.

And in the end,
with her beyond sleep,
beyond the point of resurrection,
beyond hope,
we became custodians
of her condemned house
of tired flesh.

The nurse wanted us
to stop the oxygen,
to deny her
that tiniest bit of pure sky,
to love her
by letting her
go.

And in the half-hearted name
of mercy,
we did.
And she went...
the medicine men failing us,
us angry at them for their
poked and prodded
and irradiated
failures,
not seeing how stupid
we were
to rely on them

to keep the reaper at bay,
all life stretching only so far
before falling to harvest.

But in the end
as I am left to sort through
the inheritance left
behind,
I am slowly learning
a perpetual lesson -
my mother the icon for it.
The breath
was beaten
out of her
in both the beginning and end
of her days,
but she took hold of the time in between
and made it hers.

We are as haphazard flowers,
no power over the push of the elements
nor when we will be
plucked out of our dreaming beds.
All we can do
is drink in the sun and rain,
smiling for them both,
then stand
as shining examples
to those
who need beauty most,
who wither and languish
in the shadows of death
unaware of how precious
(and quite possibly final)
each breath is.

A Moment For Jake

In your small bed
you lie surrounded
by a shower of things
soft and bright and shiny -
each one bought
with finite purpose,
the teddy bears
all looking
somewhat sad,
lined up against the crib rail
like temporary labourers;
flannel piled up
and already shrinking
with each new stretch of your bones.

So I want to give you a moment instead,
one simple moment,
this one when you lay
in your father's lap,
your feet nudging at his belly,
he a wild-haired angel
lost and dazed
in the aspect of your dreaming face.
And he smiles.

And this innocent moment
is blissfully blind,
knows no future
and had no past to be measured up to.
And so when your father smiles
it is an honest smile,
does not depend
on the gold stars you'll get
on your report card
or sports trophies.
And you do not look to it
like a barometer for his mood
or to tell you how well you did.

He smiles
simply because you are here
safe
alive
growing almost before his eyes;
because
you are impossible
the way all life
seems impossible
when we really think about it,
seems even more impossible
when we realise
that we had a clumsy hand in it.

You twist and babble in sleep
already keeping secrets from him.
A boy's jaw
sometimes learns
how to lock tight
and the world becomes full
of sullen men
pushing
and shoving
each other
with no decent words
passed between them.

And even when you have words
climbing over
a wall of teeth,
it still won't be easy.
They won't always be heard.
You will be afraid of
the weight of them sometimes,
as if they were a gun in your hand.
They will jump out in anger
and not come at all
when needed most.
They will happily

expound your ignorance
while stifling
your soft-spoken
poet heart.

Men forget
this language before language
when both man and boy
only have
the shifting features
of each other's eyes
and the curl of lips
and the furrowing
and smoothing of foreheads
and must somehow
make sense of them -
rely on the truth about us
they can reveal and betray;
this language beyond language
where,
in shared silence,
we find comfort,
where feeling transcends
the flatness of words,
where hope is something
you can touch -
even hold - in your arms.

I give you
this stopped moment
in the midst of raging time.
Here is Love,
Pure Love
asking for nothing from you,
offering everything.

Everyone Has A Poem About Cancer

Everyone has a poem about Cancer.
I heard the poet tell us
that this is what the other poet
had remarked to him
as they both listened to still another poet on stage
read their poem
about Cancer,
this being that first poet's preface
to his own poem
about Cancer.
And I thought about my poems,
a small book filled with them
like a tiny carcass
riddled with this disease
and I wondered
if I hadn't fallen
into some trap of convention,
become a cliché -
a morbid stereotype,
a trick-or-treat grim reaper,
when all I was trying to do
was flesh out the pain
put a face and a heart
and a life
to the cold statistic
death ultimately becomes.
Poems,
however,
should not be like statistics.
They should not be
counted blindly together -
their potency lost
in the raw sterility
of incomprehensible numbers.

Everyone has a poem about Cancer.
This is the most common symptom -
the one best illustrating

its deep infiltration
into our skins,
our throats,
our brains,
our lungs,
our testicles,
our prostates,
our ovaries,
our lymph nodes,
our livers,
our bowels,
our breasts,
our bones
and our blood.
It has seeped into our language -
cancerous
being a term
for anything
that eats away at the temple wall
like termites or unrequited love.
It's everywhere!
In the water;
in the air;
in my food;
in cell phones and microwaves.
Smoking can cause Cancer.
Drinking can eventually cause Cancer.
Hell, even the sun can cause Cancer these days!

Everyone has in them a poem about Cancer,
whether they are poets or not.
Everyone has a relative
or friend
or a workmate
or a lover taken down by it
or shaved too close for comfort by it;
has perhaps himself
submitted to the scalpel,
has found himself
prone for sacrifice,

entrails
picked through and prodded
like a pagan fortune-telling.
Chances are,
someone among us
has done the sick room drag-shuffle
down antiseptic corridors
saline/morphine drip
rattling in tow;
has lost their tumble-down hair,
their school girl looks;
Their appetites;
has come to know
the human body
as one
big,
weeping,
visceral
sack of damnable decay
and, on rare occasion,
near miraculous
resolve and resilience.
It doesn't help that
Medicine is in bed with it,
too much clean, pink flesh
carved out under the pretense
of prevention
or because
"We were there anyway,"
as my friend was told
when she woke to find her ovaries gone.

Yes, everyone has a poem about Cancer.
The poets are the modern equivalent
of medieval doctors
and our poems are leeches
designed to draw the poison out.
The Cancer is in us now, too,
dormant,
like a bad dream.

in broad daylight.
And although the key to happiness
sometimes
is in forgetting,
in letting go,
we have elephant memories -
the beast turning over in us
every time we reach out
for someone close
and find them gone
forever.

And when I write a poem about Cancer
I am David,
no stones to sling up at the fearsome giant,
just a handful of words,
wishing I could put a shape
to its menace
and slay it
and once and for all;
finally
put an end to all the poems
we can't stop writing
about Cancer.

The Dead of Winter

The heavens are close and pressing.
The snow falling from this
muddy December night sky
is like the wind -
felt but not seen -
betrayed by lamplight -
the quiet static
of a world between channels.
My breath is deafening.
The sidewalk is fading.
My footsteps,
holes in rice paper.
The street is a frozen river.
And I hump through
a new landscape
replete
with the monoliths
of my civilization -
machinery and utility
rendered into still life,
into statues and furniture
draped for storage.
I, too, would be overwhelmed
if not for my own
stubborn movement.
Here,
humanity is remembered
as a dream is remembered -
imperfect
and because of that,
perfect.

If I had a choice
this would be
how I'd die -
so many snowflakes
filling nose and mouth,
covering my eyes

like silver dollars -
one great sheet
over my head;
my body like some unlikely daffodil -
a surprise come Spring.

And it's okay,
I think,
to want my heaven
to be still.
All my days
are reckless
strings of moments,
each not enough
on its own,
only making sense to me
when packed together,
when piled up
like firewood -
that pile gone
every year
like it never was,
the only thing left me
to rebuild,
year after year,
each year becoming
just another big moment
to squander.
As if it were
a window breaking
or an unexpected
knock at the door,
this calm is broken
by the rumble-roar
of plodding machine
straining against
chain and harness -
a dull knife
tearing a dirty gash
in the soft fabric of winter,

the road bleeding through,
traffic beginning
to trickle along the cut
like slow poison.
And the city -
no soul to guide it -
is, as always,
a stupid golem
with no higher purpose
but to follow behind
the grinding metal beast
in its ungodly path
of resurrection.

Death, I say,
needs to be acknowledged.
I find a patch of virgin snow,
fall back,
eyes to the grieving sky,
snow filling
nose and mouth -
and there I cut an angel,
like a headstone.
Death,
I say,
needs to be acknowledged.

Bundled Ugliness

As much as we would like to,
we cannot dapple
our histories
with moonlight and romance.
By the time I had come of age
I, and all the other
freaks and geeks
who found themselves
banded together,
already knew we were
vulnerable and weak.
Grown Ups say they love
their children
but show it in funny ways -
sometimes with affection,
sometimes with rage,
sometimes with indifference.
Everything we are told
leads us to believe
that love is the putty
that binds all things,
that fills all spaces -
a product worth more than gold
in a world of broken, empty people;
in a world where
he who has the most toys wins,
in a world where we
scrabble to be king of the heap,
in a man's world.
I don't think I ever learned
what love really was,
just how it could hurt me
if I let my guard down.
We are the latest version
of a hundred generations
of men in the family.
Our legacies
hang from us -

something
handed down cold
from father to son like a gold watch
or a bad debt.

While whole schools of thought
may have been built to
explain us,
all that
mother-fucking,
father-hating
rhetoric
is lost on us,
and to be told
that we are still
struggling
to appease
and rebel against
our parents
long after we thought
          we'd left them behind -
makes us feel helpless
all over again.
And the poets
and planners
and dreamers
my friends and I
still managed
to grow up
to become
always carry a shadow -
a birthmark just under the collar,
easily revealed.
This shadow becomes
as much a part of us
as it is separate.
We learn how to conceal it
for a while
under the good suit
we put on for company -

long enough
to make it ugly
when things fall apart,
when the perfect woman
slams down the phone
once and for all
and we can't understand why
and don't see our own fault in it
and we feel our power
has been stolen from us
and so we think all women are Delilahs
to our Samson egos.

As men
we need look no further
than the mirror
behind the bar
or the reflection
in a lover's eyes
to see how
we can be bundled ugliness
sometimes;
how intimidation
is a frightening great coat
we carry on our frames;
how we can be fierce
just by our numbers.
We need to understand
how fortunate we are,
as men,
to be able to walk alone
in the sheltering blanket of night,
safe enough to ponder
Heaven, Hell and the distance between,
and not just the darkness
beyond a street lamp.

Like it or not,
we can be bullies
without even trying

and worse creatures still
when we know better
and don't stop ourselves.

The Garbage Fairy

My morning starts different -
later than expected.
The machine monster
is not bashing me out of sleep,
is not making
its lumbering,
grinding,
banging,
beeping,
rumbling way
up my alley,
denting can
and busting bottle
as it goes.

And this is the extent
of my relation
to my refuse -
a waking nightmare,
like all nightmares,
dealing with my crap for me
in spite of me,
then lost
as the day settles into
yet another kind of sleep.

As a society
we have relegated
our trash
to the realm of fairies -
figured we could
leave it out and as if magic,
as if pulled teeth
or virgin sacrifice,
it would disappear,
our hand hardly dirtied.
No surprise.
We have done the same with our money

bankers and CGAs
like leprechauns
lining their pockets
and leaving us
scant handfuls
of lucky charms
to try wishing on.

And we have done the same
with our morality:
lawmakers laughing
when we cry for justice,
Justice bought and sold
and bartered for,
but never truly won.

Money,
law
and garbage -
all too big.
All too dirty.

Well, ladies and gentlemen,
today the garbage fairy is on strike
and turned or sleeping heads
will not evoke him.
His morning
begins different, too:
His coffee,
sitting warm and undisturbed in his belly,
is not yanked up
by the stench of my kitchen catcher -
contents full,
rotten long before
it ever hits the curb.
He needs no gloves
to hoist a picket sign.
His lawn chair
is not great for his back;
but at least he's sitting,

smiling,
I imagine,
truly king of the heap,
knowing his kingdom grows
with every passing moment,
each moment
being
another carton assembled,
another purchase,
another expiry date,
another Big Mac wrapped,
another diaper soiled,
another samosa bagged,
another newspaper,
another coffee to go,
another condom filled.

It is all money in the bank to him,
coffers beyond brimming.

But it is the children
who truly inherit the apathy,
being both the product
and the perpetuation of it.
They will ball up
and toss away
their own tomorrows
unaware of how it all comes back
the way karma always does.

A little boy
threw down his juice box.
It bounced as hollow
on the sidewalk
as a bad promise.

And as grown-ups
gaggled around him like geese,
his mother feigned outrage,
humiliated,

because everyone knows
it's never a bad kid
just bad parents.
He,
like a god incensed
at the impudence
of his own angels,
looked up and down -
the filth
swirling about
his bandy legs -
and asked,
"But why?
This is the city."

Horrified
as I was -
as we all were -
one look
at this grimy landscape
of human waste and discard
and we had no argument.

Indeed,
this
is
the city -
the hottest day of the year
beating down
relentless,
parching the dusty skin of July
then kicking it up
all over August
like a cat trying to cover its business,
turning our trash cans
into cooking pots;
stewing up our table scraps,
our back lanes
becoming soup kitchens
for racoons and skunks

and seagulls;
garbage bags
busting their putrid guts
wasps buzzing chaos,
over the spoils;
the chicken bones
and orange peels
like ironic smiles;
a billion shopping trips
otherwise forgotten
but for a few
billowing,
rattling
grocery bag spooks
haunting the limbs of trees,
hanging
dangling
the way condemned men do;
those six pack rings
ducks take to wearing
like costume necklaces
until the swell of life
meets the strangle of death
slow and flapping
and final on a park green -
the last heartbreaking
signs of struggle
over
before
the great certainty of winter
(and all the glorious implications
of flight held in that season)
can be realised;
cars with lone drivers on bottlenecked bridges;
the litter of a fast food joint
becoming its best advertising;
all the poems
double-spaced
and single-sided
revised

and rejected
a half-dozen times...

Three hundred and forty
tons of garbage a day
this city makes.
That's
one hundred,
twenty-four
thousand,
one hundred
tons a year.
And our answer is to
dig a hole and bury it
like pirates' gold.
And so a landfill in Surrey
lies at the end
of the garbage man's rainbow;
his bounty safe there,
him knowing for sure
that no one ever wants to lay claim to it.
He sits in the sweltering,
spoiling sun
and patiently waits,
and laughs
and laughs
and laughs.

*This poem was written after the 1997 Vancouver garbage strike
which lasted 5 weeks - the second largest such strike in the city's
history.*

Likely It'll Happen

There's a rock on the sidewalk
in front of a plate glass window
in an angry neighborhood.
Even I want to throw it.
Some things seem inevitable,
like poor kids throwing rocks
at passing trains,
like great cosmic hands
throwing comets at dinosaurs.

My street is
a kaleidoscope
of colour,
dialect,
smell.
I am the minority,
larger than
my life feels,
lumbering,
visible,
white.

Radios,
dogs
and foul language,
sirens and car horns;
teeming,
drunk,
struggling,
tired,
this human stew
all boils down
to garbage in the gutters,
a discarded shoe,
a pair of soiled underwear,
and a million used condoms -
all stories never told.

We all come into this world
with enough senses
to feel what lies around us,
what covers over us,
what suffocates us.
Wealth has found
more than enough ways
to keep itself exclusive
on my street,
in my neighborhood,
unattainable
like the million names of God
no one really comprehends.
Suburbia lays its foundations
in the pit of the city's bowels -
big expensive boots
stamp out the wildflowers
growing through the cracks.
Choosing
concrete and poverty
for your home
just doesn't make sense
to we who have no such choices,
always bartering for our happiness,
never being able to afford to buy it.

I tremble
with the humiliating,
certain
belief
that I have
no control
over
my own
body,
mind,
or life,
like a repeat victim;
like frustration and a voice
not taken seriously;

like when Liberty and Justice
are both blind;
when you can't read;
when you can't work
or when your work ain't considered
worth the cost of the materials
let alone
your time
or your passion;
when your pockets are stuffed full
of magic beans
and crazy dreams
but little else;
and when those who have
still want more from you
despite your constant insistence
that there is nothing more to give;
when your tongue greets strangers
with words found stranger still;
when you can't stop thoughts
from spilling out your head.
and onto the street around you
fluid and roiling
a kind of nausea.
A body
can only take
being rag-doll rattled around
like that for so long,
can only stand witness
to all that outrage
for so long.
Instinctively,
inevitably,
a hand will clench up...
Remember
how we used to play
"Paper, Scissors, Rock"
when we needed to settle things?
Rocks carried weight
back then.

There's a rock on the sidewalk
in front of a plate glass window.
Even I want to throw it.
Some things just seem inevitable,
like paper always beating rock.

When Something Happened

Something great happened to me today -
for once
luck
on my side,
the impossible happening:
the sky falling
and a sunny chunk of it
dropping in my lap...

And the first person
I wanted to call
was my mother -
the prodigal son
wanting to reassure her
he's making good,
that he ain't all jester body
and fanciful head,
reassuring
himself
at the same time.

But my mother is dead.
Memory seeps in
like a winter draft.

My mother is dead
eight months now,
her estate divided,
her ashes a dusty blanket
over my father's grave.
Eight months
of grieving
and survival
and countless moments like this
where my bright triumphs
are lost
to a dull ache
overwhelming...

I can never find the words
to fully describe this,
not to someone who's never
gone through it,
their losses
being confined
to puppies
or parakeets
or maybe a grandmother.
Opening up this subject
makes the air go heavy
like the pregnant quiet
before a midsummer storm
and all we can think about
is hiding from it,
forgetting -
in this panic -
how good the rain can feel,
how necessary it is.

And when my friends
complain about their families
all I can do is
shake my head,
thinking that it's all
so stupid,
that such squabbling
is what they will regret most,
last words
being the only things
to really last forever,
"I love you,"
or
"I'm sorry,"
seldom part of the vocabulary.

My mother's children
have truly become
a litter:
Us scattered over

troubled distances
as if so much loose paper,
me feeling
the most bedraggled,
the least important,
my chicken little days
blowing me higgledy-piggledy
from poem to poem,
from daydream to pitfall,
from pay cheque to last call.

There is space between us -
and age
and politics
and experience
that fills up
all the awkward,
frequent
gaps
in our conversations
like mortar.

We have learned
different languages;
theirs seemingly
a steady lineage of words
which makes me think
way farther ahead
than I want to -
words like 'children"
and 'mortgage"
and "retirement";
a word like "security" being,
for them,
full of numbers
and percentages
and interest rates;
for me;
a good lock on the door
or maybe a neighbor I can trust.

My mother spoke a more subtle dialect -
one of blood and history,
her purpose
not to make a point
but a connection,
passing on
story and anecdote
from brother
to brother
to sister,
closing that distance,
seeing some reason
for family unity
we didn't
that I still
can't always see the importance of,
my brother and sister
taking up the cause
in her place,
snapping photographs,
tapping out email,
offering me a home
to come home to
for all those proper holidays,
more contact
in these last few hurting months
than ever before.
And from that
my brother and I
have maybe become the closest,
having never really known each other before,
him more of a rumor
haunting knick-knacks
in my childhood house and head,
his name sometimes lilting and a little regretful
in my mother's throat.
He is a kind of pre-history,
surfacing from the flatness of photography,
beyond my first memories
when my parents were

different,
younger
people
driven by
different,
bigger
dreams
and fears.

My brother
can remember more
than my father
as a bellowing old man.
He can remember
a time
long ago
in a barn
in private
when my father
broke down
saying he was afraid
of being
left alone.

And this,
my brother and I have discovered,
is a fear
passed down through generations:
his wife
defining his future
my girlfriend
softly filling my days,
both of us
now orphans.

And he went to call mom too,
just the other day,
and knows
this mute rage,
and still carries

a lot of shit
on his shoulders
and as if I actually
know something,
I told him,
"Well, it depends
on what you think Death is…
If the light goes out
and that's it,
then don't worry about it,
because she isn't.
And if you believe
the soul persists,
romps through green pastures,
learns to play the harp,
then keep talking."
It's why I keep a journal
or write poetry -
the whisper of pen on paper,
a hushed intimation
to my own audience of angels,
to my own troubled head,
to get me through the day,
the day full of people left alone
and
things
left
unsaid.

Mill Town Gunslinger

I come back
to my hometown
always a prodigal son -
full of stories,
fully believing my own press
about a bigger,
better
world
beyond the shadowy edges of town
and me taking it by the balls.

I come back
and head straight for the bar
just like a gunslinger would
and I feel like a gunslinger,
The whole town wanting a piece of me,
me wanting
to lay flowers
over my memories,
to yank up
my trip-over roots
and be rid of this place.

But it's never that easy.

The past
does not like to lie
buried and forgotten
and I am not
vagabond enough
to put
emotional distance
between me and it.
History cannot sleep
unless it is understood
and appreciated.
I know how it feels.

So I find a table,
back to the wall,
fingers curled around my drink,
and I take in the ambience
of this dirty
little
one-horse town.

The pulp mill,
always close,
rumbles day and night,
a brilliant,
stinking city
unto itself,
feeding and forsaking
the scurrying flesh
which is
its blood and waste,
its profit and loss,
its heart and soul.

And the town nestles
alongside of it,
drinking its foul water,
breathing its stench,
raising children
to tend to it,
building houses in its shadow,
building a church to count
blessings in.
And the bingo/banquet hall
at the top of the hill
is where they dream
bigger than themselves
for a little while,
but where life
is ultimately summed up
by a push broom
at the end of the night.

And of course
they built this bar,
where the men around me
seem as permanent and run down
as the carpet
and not as big as I remember
and older
and their wisdom spews haphazard
in clumps of pickled egg and beer,
and in the "achy breaky heart"
of darkness
which is this place
and always was,
I think I know why
I couldn't wait to leave.

The door cracks open
and what could have been my life
walks in and pulls up the same chair
he always sits in,
and there is no word of greeting
when he slaps down
his smokes
in front of him,
and the beer just comes
and the money just slides away.

And these men
and sons of men
one moment swagger
like they own the town
and the next
curse the town that owns them
and something unspoken says
that when time
has a dollar figure
sweat has a price too
and when your life is counted
in dollars and hours
it always comes up short.

But they embrace the work,
take pride in their precision,
gather
in fraternities
and brotherhoods,
rally at the front gate
kick dirt up
in the face of the machine
every now and then.

They do this
until they feel the swell
and stiffening
of their shoulders
in painful resignation,
but by then,
the hours are years
and if you count off
enough of them
they give you a gold watch
and you get to buy an RV
or move to Florida for the winter.

And all the things
collected
over the years:
a family,
a home,
a front lawn,
a backyard -
are
more than most
big city
slingers
like me
will ever have.
I forget that,
forget how I once wanted all that,
how maybe I still do,
how maybe

I ran away
because
I was scared
or jealous.
All I know is that
I wanted more
from my own dreams,
more than to meet my end
face down in the mud
just like my father did,
my son sleeping through
the pointless afternoon
dreaming of shining towers
just like I did.

All I know is that
I almost
take comfort
in being alone
in the city
and no one cares
if I am
or judges me
on my profession
or my solitude -
chosen or not.

Yet I come back
to my hometown
looking to tear up
my planted feet,
to discard my connection
to the brave,
angry,
committed,
suffering,
human bed
I grew from.
For this
I truly am a fool.

The Dishwasher's Hour

When the last patron
has stepped out the door
shaking his little mints
in his loose, fat fists,
hardly remembering his dishes
when really they are
the whole reason
he ate out:
so that someone else
would do them for him.
This is when the dishwasher
does his most important work,
not the catch-up
keep up
so what work
of two-for-one pasta night
dinners rushes,
but the end of the night
put everything in its right
        place
clean slate
last dirty plate
kind of work.
Blessed is this hour,
the longest one tonight,
last in a line of so many
other thankless tonights
that make up my dismal career.

The waitress counts out her cash.
Her boyfriend owns a muscle car
and waits for her.
If the grill cook and I like him,
he sits in the dining room,
feet up on a chair,
her vacuuming under him.
If we don't, he sits in his car,
Metallica blowing his speakers.

This hour is rung in
with the clang of pots
and the rush of water.
My hands are dead white fish
hanging from my elbows.
I swear at the sous-chef
and his incompetence -
a good cook would not leave
this crap behind
for me to bloody my knuckles on.
The air is burnt meat sauce,
rotting lettuce
dish soap
and hot water.
This boiled down American dream
is a fog I nearly choke on,
have to wash out of my hair,
pick out of my nose
and scrape off my teeth.

The dumpster out back
must be a precious thing.
The owner keeps it locked up
and out of sight.
It is my refuge,
my momentary escape.

I drag my bent-back,
grease-spackled
sorry ass
out to it every night.
In tow behind me
is the bundled remains of the day -
the bone cut from the flesh,
the skin cut from the flesh,
the fat from the flesh,
all the trimmings
because no one eats the trimmings,
all the hard bits
that gravy can't soften,

the paper napkins
stained with politeness -
the sour remains of the day.

The night is fresh and clean,
not like detergent,
more like inspiration.
The city quiets down
long enough
for me to do my work in peace
and I can finally
hear my own thoughts again.

The waitress is an actress
and the dishwasher is a poet.
You are anything but the uniform
they make you wear.
The world is your oyster
and it sure the fuck
won't be Oysters Rockefeller.
When you are young
this kind of job
is gas in the car,
smoke in your lungs,
beer down the front of your shirt,
but definitely not forever.
But the distance
between now and forever
fills a lot of days.
The dishwasher
is now a health care worker
but still a poet at heart.
The waitress was smart enough
to figure out
it was okay to be a waitress
and let the theatre
swallow up her place on-stage
with no regrets.
The poet still lugs around
a lot of garbage.

Back under the dumpster lid,
not concerned with career choices,
the maggots are living high
off our refuse.
Everything comes to them.
My hour becomes theirs.

Lady Hare Holding Greyhound

***A poem for Sophie Ryder's statue, "Lady Hare Holding Dog"
which stood for a while on the seawall in Vancouver, BC.***

The foundation
she once stood on
cradling him,
is a grey concrete,
inhuman
clear-cut;
a desolate summit
to the rich green mound of grass -
this:
   a thankless gravestone
with no epitaph
to pay tribute to them,
to her,
to the loss I am feeling,
to that artist's skill when she shaped the two of them,
the hound's draped surrender
at the hands of his victim,
he, so small compared to her -
she, a truly statuesque beauty:
quick-thinking rabbit head
on full-figured woman body.
and despite the tough, molten metal of their hides
and the blindness of her eyes
in this poor,
sculpted
excuse for a brier patch,
she was the best of humanity
and something I had counted on -
her absence
just one more disappointment.

Hers was the courage to stave off
the dog-eat-doe delusions
of this monstrous city
and these mad days -
an example for fear mongers

and nations
and neighbors
and families
all turning on one another.

Ignoring the treacherous stink of canine,
she would lean in and whisper to him:
"It's alright.
So what if you are a dog?
I still love you."
She must have known the risk
of holding her enemy so close
despite the axiom
that that's just where you want him.

Perhaps she remembered
her own run-in with the tortoise
and it would make her smile
to think of how foolish and prideful
she must have been
for thinking she could outrun the inevitable.

And in this mean world
of hard angles
and broken asphalt
at what seems to be the end
of my own run-ragged race,
I came here looking for them,
my back slumped,
tail between my legs, too,
hoping to return to the garden
where the lion lays down with the lamb
and the rabbit comforts the greyhound
and found them gone instead,
trampled under construction boot,
scared off by heavy machines
that chew up compassion
and spit it out as cement.

That First Quiet Year

O.E. Rölvaag noted in his book "Giants In the Earth" that European settlers agreed that there were neither bird nor insect life on the American prairie (traditional territory of the Dakota First Nation) with the exception of the mosquitos the first year they came.

The sky was empty,
the land barren
and too big to fully comprehend
without going mad from the loneliness.
The journey was mostly in the head,
words jarring and foreign
and lost in the expanse -
no mountains to return them to you.
Besides,
what was there to talk about?
The past
something that had to be pushed down,
the future
as uncertain and terrifying as the next hill,
the present,
flat and unremarkable.

In that first year
only the wind spoke
through the vocal cords of prairie grass,
drummed against the canvas of tent flaps
and stone-washed sheets laundered in the sun.
Much of the breathing life there was
came with them
tethered and plodding,
tired and humbled.

I found this as no more than a footnote,
as if history itself
were trying to forget
how vacant and hopeless
those beginning times were.

Nature went into hiding -
the jack rabbits
watching from behind tall grass,
knowing wagon wheels
longed for highways
to speed along,
ancient romping paths
cut short,
Death would gleam
and bear down on them
at a hundred unnecessary miles an hour.

The prairie dogs
hunched in their warrens,
hoof beats
pounding like jackhammers,
their homes torn up
to make way for concrete,
foundations dug deep
to support pointless high-rises
scraping the virgin sky.

The hawks and gulls
kept themselves grounded,
shuddering
at the thought of
fire from below,
at the thought of
shiny metal contraptions
clumsily imitating flight
but never grace,
greasy trails of smoke
left behind
to somehow navigate through.

And the insects -
the true scrabbling kings
of this place
since time immemorial,
vanished,

knowing they stood
no chance
under hand
or boot heel.

But most of all,
it was the white men themselves
who paralysed them all with fear,
already spectres
in their new cities of the dead -
ghosts in the making.
Their imposed order
made no sense,
uprooting trees
and wildflowers
and natural beauty
for manicured parks
with jungle gyms
where no one ever went,
leaving them for nature
to tear apart again
in its own
slow,
sad
way;
squaring off space
so getting from here to there
meant going first
there,
then there,
then there;
standing in line,
buying land
then leaving it empty;
killing in anger;
laughing in spite;
drinking to forget;
loving out of context;
dying from disillusion.

The animals lay in waiting
that first long year,
hoping with all their fluttering hearts
that we were nothing but a bad dream,
that we'd simply go away,
that maybe,
in our blindness,
we'd fall
over the edge
of our own frontier.

A Day Counted in Crows

This bleak, tempestuous day is counted
on the pendulum swing of
East Vancouver crow flight.

This morning they fought the wind all the way,
looking more like fall leaves
half asleep with empty bellies
pushed and shoved,
lifted and thrown,
down made up
true made false.
They surfed the madcap sea of sky
with the grace of a discarded paper plate,
and yet their caws sounded like belly laughter
and they pressed on,
confused, perhaps,
but seemingly unafraid.

Tonight, the wing beat home is sure
and the path home is arrow straight.
Tonight the wind
is just a good story
to whisper into the crook of their wings
as they hunker down
after a day
of feasting
in overflowing dumpsters
of boundless extravagance.
They fight over a french-fry
or maybe a discarded dinner roll,
but it still ends well -
small disputes
lost in the cacophony of mass, general complaint.

The rain is a done deal
and on its way.
Sleep is hard earned.
Life is hard earned.

A Sparrow Death

It was my poet friend Andrew,
who first saw it -
the tiny carcass
dangling in the November air.
He seems to
have a way of
spotting these things,
as if Death
crouches on his shoulder
and points them out;
hard for me to take sometimes,
me always trying to catch
the best of the day,
a little afraid of Death
despite my own suspicions
that it's just a trick
the soul uses
to shake off a body.

I had never seen it.
Through this door
at least a dozen times now
and I'd never looked up there.
Now I couldn't turn away,
rain dropping on my head,
shoulders sagging
under my boxed and bundled life.
Just under the eaves
in what would have been
a good place for birds -
out of the weather,
out of the reach of cats
and curious children -
a sparrow drooped
like a rotten pear -
a straw-boned
and feather-dusted
skin bag of body.

The cause of its demise
was obvious
but nonetheless
horrific,
head and neck caught
between a beam
and a straight-edged
piece of tin -
cut sharp -
the welfare
of no sparrow in mind.

Nothing made any sense -
beside this corpse
a hole easily big enough
to slip in and out of;
within,
a dry nest of twigs
and sparrow down
to call home -
more than I had at that moment.

Christ!
He's committed suicide,
I thought to myself,
going out simple,
as easy
as succumbing to gravity.
And I thought,
Man it's got to be tough out there
if even the birds have given up hope.
I mean,
it ain't beyond
the realm of possibility,
really.
Lemmings off themselves
(although I've heard
the Disney ones were pushed).
Maybe the dreams I have -
the ones I pray for

before sleep -
are further
from reality
than I guessed.
Maybe
the power to rise
up above
the stink and filth
of these dull sidewalks
and these ugly walls
and these blind alleys
and these garbage heaps
and these small and frequent
scenes of human pain
and rage
and disappointment
is not such a great power
after all.
And maybe
the bird
gave up on the big dream
all birds are supposed to
strive for and buy into,
one day realizing
that he was never going to
live up to
that "golden-goose-egg" ideal,
but by then
it was too late to make other plans.

Or perhaps it was
just some kind of accident -
the freak kind -
like when office workers
lynch themselves
with their ties
trapped
in their top desk drawers.
Human magic
can be a dangerous thing,

the cryptic equations
of power
and speed
and height
and distance
and inertia
combined
with the irrefutable truth
of glass
and concrete
and steel
and fire
and steam
enough to baffle most of us.
And living in an age
so full of wonder and distraction
we forget
the dangers
these things
all still possess:
Stepping on a crack -
then falling -
probably did break
some mother's back;
walking under a ladder
is unlucky
when the guy
standing on it
drops his hammer.
Cars crash,
knives cut,
guns go off
in unsteady hands,
and sparrows
and starlings
and swallows
and pigeons
and crows
all live in this
alongside us

and if we trip over
and bump into
and stand under
a walk in front of
danger all the time
why wouldn't they?

And to those
who don't linger much
on matters
like dead sparrows
or lunatic poets
this poem
might seem pointless,
but the questions
behind its inception
are so fundamental
they've nearly brought
two good friends to blows:
Are we animals
who dream ourselves more,
or are we gods
feeling guilty
for acting less than gods?
It's fitting
that Andrew be here,
in the poem.
After all,
it's he and I
who natter
and scrap
and scream at one another
over this very subject
time and ungainly time again;
he and I who've
found this to be
the unsettling joke
between us,
the way it creeps into
our conversations

when we least expect it,
turning pleasantries
into jagged,
impassioned affairs
of honour
and dignity
and intellect.

And while he and I talk,
each stubbornly refusing
to give in to the other
(except for that time
I let it slip
that we might be animals,
but I was drunk
and say a lot of crazy things
when I'm drunk).
While he and I talk
there are whole populations
who have given up the rhetoric
centuries ago,
who carry their convictions
deep in their veins;
who have bled
and burned
for them;
who,
like me,
do not always
have the words
when they come to the table;
or who have just enough words
to encompass their own beliefs,
seeing no practical need
for any more.

And to what end
do we battle -
To determine
whether

psychology
or zoology
will be the dogma
we let guide us
and beyond that
to decide
whether we are
infinite souls
or finite sadness?

It all seems trivial
when set beside
the great travesty
that is a sparrow's death.

To my friend,
Andrew,
I propose
a truce
to our silly religious war.
There are
far more important skirmishes
to be fought
and the troops
must not be divided.

History
is the story
of the comings
and goings
of things
and he and I have a place in it:
our part
writing the testimony
of the living moment
and the last breath
as best we can.

He must
keep looking for small deaths.

They are
as much the story of life
as the beating heart
and the raging voice,
and there must be room made
for both of us
to dream bigger and smaller
than ourselves,
because
our opinions are the only things
we give away freely
while still
holding onto tightly.
And our bloody,
human history
has proven
that not even death
can change that.

This Brilliant Day

This brilliant day
is all about defiance
and grand revolution
and the true revolutionaries
are the daffodils
who rear
their fearsome heads
year after year,
our mowers and shears
toothless
like old men.
And the legions of grass
stand silent
and resilient,
blades
pointed to the blue sky,
knowing only
their purpose
of growing as tall
as they can
in the short span of time
they are offered.

And I think I understand
what Bradbury was doing
with his
"dandelion wine" -
distilling spring and summer,
then bottling it
for sullen,
weathered-in winter days -
fuel for future rebellions.

"Pop" goes the cork
and a million
bright-faced flowers
rage again
against

the conformity
of cut and dry
human mentality,
scream chaos
and smile,
bowing only
to the breeze.

And I go back
to when I was once the butcher,
red-faced,
brow beading sweat,
belly
hard up
against the machine,
back and body
full to it,
the struggle
epic
and endless
and worth
a week's allowance;
the front lawn
at last
laid waste,
my sneakers
and blue jeans
smeared with its blood,
my veins throbbing
in my neck,
my chest heaving,
my victory
soon enough
forgotten,
the lawn sprouting up
almost in my wake -
defiant
like a young boy,
like a summer day.

Party Like It's the End of the World

Today feels like
the day after
the "End of The World" party.

The morning is too real.

Sunlight chisels the landscape,
honing detail razor-sharp.
Sound is like a phonebook
upside the head
and the breakfast joints
are jumping
with shaky fingers
and pale faces,
kicking back cancer
with caffeine chasers.

Talk is on how
we jimmied the lock
on Pandora's box
and let chaos loose
last night.

Whether we planned
to live forever
or die tomorrow,
we carried on the same.
We are people
full of unfinished todays
and indebted tomorrows
and last night
it was to hell with it all
as we bojangled along
sidewalks of trouble
pushed by the moon
and the gut-emptiness
of desperation and hard luck.

We lashed out wild
at invisible giants
but hit home,
family
and friends instead.

And so today
our churches are full
of silent repentance,
Shame,
the incense hanging...

and our beds are full
of fitful sadness sleeping,
and we are afraid
to wake
to remember
how we hurt the only people
who ever
truly took us in,

and we still taste
and smell the strangers
gone from the sheets beside us
and feel foolish for believing
we could cure
lifetime's worth of loneliness
in just one night,

and the toilets
are rank
with red wine
as a week of upheaval
finally shows itself
for what it is,

and I walk through
the Saturday night litter
of Sunday morning,
the condoms,

the socks stiff with glue,
the needles,
the pipes
and paraphernalia
are party favors for the apocalypse,

and the day will drag on
in spite of
our stopped hearts,
and dusk will come again
like a slow,
certain
blindness,
and whether we planned
to live forever
or die tomorrow
what we have done
and seen
will never be enough,
and we will rail against
ourselves
one more time.

My part of town
knows how to do it right -
how to party
like it's the end of the world.